# Ladybug Puppet

**written by Jay Dale**

photography by Ned Meldrum

Here is my ladybug puppet.

This is for your ladybug puppet.

2 paper plates

stapler

red paint

black paper

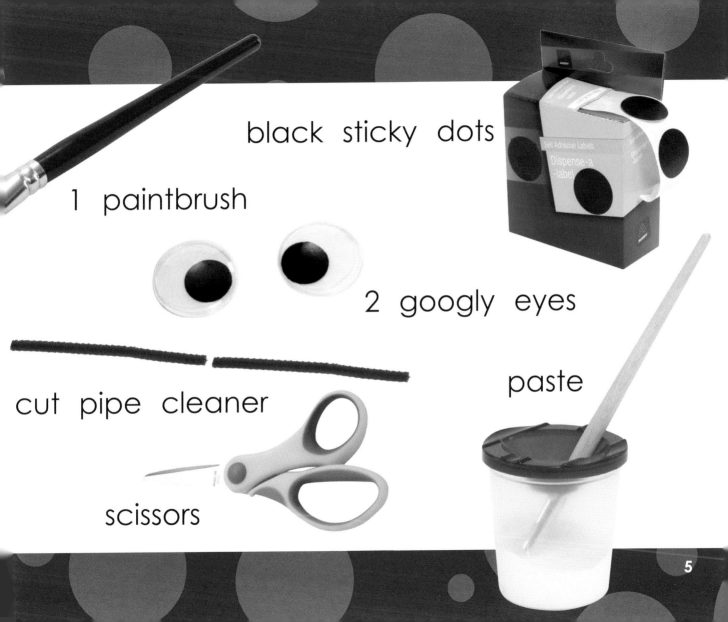

black sticky dots

1 paintbrush

2 googly eyes

cut pipe cleaner

paste

scissors

5

Here are the paper plates.

Cut a paper plate like this.

The paper plates go like this.

This is for your hand.

Cut the paper like this.

Here are the legs.

The legs go here.

Here is the red paint.

Here is the paintbrush.

The red paint goes here.

Cut the black paper like this.

The black paper goes here.

Here are the eyes.

The eyes go here.

Here are the black dots.

The dots go here.

1, 2, 3.

1, 2, 3.

Here are the pipe cleaners.

The pipe cleaners go here.

Here is your ladybug puppet.